curious about

# DRAGO

T0249309

BY GINA KAMMER

# What are you

# curious about?

CHAPTER THREE

## Finding Dragons
PAGE
**16**

Curious About is published
by Amicus
P.O. Box 227
Mankato, MN 56002
www.amicuspublishing.us

Editor: Marysa Storm
Series Designer: Kathleen Petelinsek
Book Designer: Catherine Berthiaume
Photo researcher: Bridget Prehn

Library of Congress Cataloging-in-Publication Data
Names: Kammer, Gina, author.
Title: Curious about dragons / by Gina Kammer.
Description: Mankato, MN : Amicus, 2023. | Series:
Curious about mythical creatures | Includes bibliographical
references and index. | Audience: Ages 6–9 | Audience:
Grades 2–3 | Summary: "Surveys the legends and
folklore about dragon habitat, appearance, and behavior
in a fun question-and-answer format that reinforces inquiry-
based learning for early elementary-age readers. A Stay
Curious! Learn More feature models research skills and
doubles as a mini media literacy lesson. Includes simple
infographics, glossary, and index"– Provided by publisher.
Identifiers: LCCN 2020001135 (print) | LCCN 2020001136
(ebook) | ISBN 9781645491262 (library binding) | ISBN
9781681526935 (paperback) | ISBN 9781645491682 (pdf)
Subjects: LCSH: Dragons–Juvenile literature.
Classification: LCC GR830.D7 K36 2021 (print) | LCC
GR830.D7 (ebook) | DDC 398.24/54–dc23
LC record available at https://lccn.loc.gov/2020001135
LC ebook record available at https://lccn.loc.gov/2020001136

Photos © Shutterstock / Valentyna Chukhlyebova 1, 7 (Western);
iStock / ZU_09 4–5; Shutterstock / Aaron Lim 6; Shutterstock
/ Bodor Tivadar 7 (Hydra); Shutterstock / Graphic Compressor
7 (Ouroboros); Wikimedia Commons / British Museum 7
(Xiuhcoatl); Shutterstock / tratong 7 (Watatsumi); Alamy /
Danita Delimont 8–9; Shutterstock / Anton Starikov 11 (left);
iStock / Picture Partners 11 (middle); Shutterstock / WICHAI
WONGJONGGAIHAN 11 (right); Shutterstock / Melkor3D
12–13; Shutterstock / Suwit Luangpipatsorn 14–15; iStock /
ewg3D 16–17; Shutterstock / GUDKOV ANDREY 19 (top);
Getty / barbaraaaa 19 (sea dragon); Shutterstock / ifong 19
(bearded dragon); Shutterstock / Hintau Aliaksei 19 (dragonflies);
Shutterstock / Anastelfy 20; Shutterstock / lian_2011 21;
Shutterstock / TRONIN ANDREI 22–23

# CHAPTER ONE

# Are dragons real?

All around the world, people have told stories about dragons. These creatures came in many forms. The best-known dragon **legends** are from Europe and Asia. But all we have are stories. No one has found **proof** that dragons ever existed.

The Old English story of Beowulf has the hero battle a dragon.

# What do dragons look like?

Most dragons are shown with big, sharp teeth.

Dragons are usually scaly **reptiles**. They look like big snakes or lizards. Most have wings and strong tails. Some have claws like eagles. They can be huge, tiny, or change sizes. In one legend from China, a dragon shrinks. It gets so small it fits in a rice bowl.

**WESTERN
(EUROPEAN)**

**HYDRA
(GREEK)**

**OUROBOROS
(EGYPTIAN)**

**XIUHCOATL
(AZTEC FIRE SERPENT)**

**WATATSUMI
(JAPANESE)**

Breathing fire is just one of a dragon's possible powers.

# What magic powers do dragons have?

In legends, dragons can fly and breathe fire. Some can breathe ice or **venom**. Some change shape or change the weather. Wingless dragons seem to swim through the air. They stay up using the magic of a bump on their heads.

# CHAPTER TWO

# How long do dragons live?

Dragons can live thousands of years. They hatch from eggs as babies. Then they keep growing bigger. They just need enough food or magic. Unless they are killed, some dragons may live forever!

Korean legends say dragons caught orbs to give them magic powers.

## COMPARING SIZES
### How big are dragon eggs?

small dragon egg – 0.5 inches (1 cm)

chicken egg – 2.5 inches (6 cm)

ostrich egg – 6 inches (15 cm)

dragon egg – 12 inches (30 cm)

# What do dragons like to do?

Dragons are known for hoarding treasure.

Dragons like to eat. Hungry dragons eat lots of meat. Big dragons might eat whole cows! But more than anything, dragons love **treasure**. With full bellies, they sleep on piles of gold or jewels. They keep the treasure safe. Don't wake a dragon!

# Are dragons friendly?

In some legends, dragons are helpful. They bring rain that helps plants grow. But these dragons can also cause floods or storms. Angry dragons may destroy cities. They won't share their treasure, either! A dragon might spit fire at thieves.

Many places have dragon statues.

# CHAPTER THREE

# Where do dragons live?

Dragons live in places that are hard to reach. Western dragons live alone in caves and on mountains. Dragons from Asia can live in the ocean or water. Some have castles under water! Others live in rain clouds.

**Dragons were thought to live in caves and other hard-to-reach places.**

# What else could a dragon be?

People have found some real animals that seem like dragons. Komodo dragons are big lizards. They can grow up to 10 feet (3 m) long.

Long ago, people found dinosaur bones. People didn't know about dinosaurs yet. People probably thought they were dragon bones!

Komodo dragons live on five small islands in Indonesia.

## OTHER ANIMALS

People have named other animals after dragons. Can you guess why?

sea dragons

bearded dragons

dragonflies

# Could you train a dragon?

In legends, some dragons are smart and friendly. They are also dangerous. Dragons with so much power aren't easy to train. But smart dragons like word games. Talk to a dragon. It might be your best chance to get a dragon to do what you want. Be polite!

Perhaps wizards would
have the best chance of
training dragons!

## ASK MORE QUESTIONS

**What other things could be mistaken for dragons?**

**What stories have people told about dragons?**

**Try a BIG QUESTION: Why did people come up with dragons in the first place?**

## SEARCH FOR ANSWERS

**Search the library catalog or the Internet.**
A librarian, teacher, or parent can help you.

**Using Keywords**
Find the looking glass.

**Keywords are the most important words in your question.**

**If you want to know about:**

- other animals that are like dragons, type:
  ANIMALS LIKE DRAGONS
- dragons in legends, type:
  DRAGON LEGENDS

# FIND GOOD SOURCES

## Here are some good, safe sources you can use in your research.
An adult can help you find more.

## Books
**Dragons** by Marty Erickson, 2022.

**A First Look at Dragons** by Emma Carlson-Berne, 2021.

## Internet Sites
**Planet Earth II: Flying Dragons Of the Jungle**
https://thekidshouldseethis.com/post/flying-dragons-of-the-jungle-planet-earth-ii-bbc
BBC is public television in Britain. It has news and information on many topics.

**PBS: What Dragons Say about Us**
https://pbs.org/video/what-dragons-say-about-us-zowt4u/
PBS is public television. Public television has great learning videos without many ads.

Every effort has been made to ensure that these websites are appropriate for children. However, because of the nature of the Internet, it is impossible to guarantee that these sites will remain active indefinitely or that their contents will not be altered.

# SHARE AND TAKE ACTION

## Go to a zoo and learn about what makes each animal different.
Think about what they need to survive.

## Find an old image of a dragon.
Compare how it looks similar to or different from dragons in books and movies today.

## Draw your own type of dragon and write a story about it.
Show it to your family or friends and tell them why you chose that type.

# GLOSSARY

**legends** Stories from the past that may or may not be true but cannot be checked.

**proof** Evidence of something.

**reptiles** Animals that are covered in scales, usually lay eggs, and are cold-blooded.

**treasure** Something that is very special and valuable.

**venom** A poison that an animal uses to kill or injure another animal by biting or stinging.

# INDEX

## About the Author

Gina Kammer grew up writing and illustrating her own stories. Now she edits children's books and writes for all ages. She likes to read fantasy and medieval literature. She also enjoys traveling, oil painting, archery, and snuggling her grumpy bunny. She lives in Minnesota.